KV-510-190

Withdrawn From Stock
Dublin City Public Libraries

Be Happy!
A Little Book of Mindfulness

written by
Maddy Bard

illustrated by
Emma Dodd

templar
books

Be Happy

Hucky and Buzz love to run in the park
and feel the grass under their paws.
What do you like to do?

Be Thankful

Hucky and Buzz appreciate the little things.

Look at the beautiful world around you.

What are you thankful for?

Be Kind

Kindness makes everyone feel better and can be shown in lots of different ways. What kind things can you do?

Show Love

Being loved is a happy feeling.
It makes us feel warm inside.
Give someone a big hug
to show them that you care!

Breathe

Sometimes Hucky and Buzz sit quietly
and listen to the sound of their breathing.

Put your hand on your tummy and breathe in slowly
through your nose, then out through your mouth.
How does it make you feel?

Believe in Yourself
With self-confidence,
you can do amazing things!

Feel Your Feelings

Sometimes it's OK not to feel OK.

Talk to Someone

When Hucky and Buzz are worried or sad,
they talk to each other.

Stay Positive

You never know what will happen tomorrow – maybe something great! Hucky and Buzz enjoy the surprises each day brings.

Keep Busy

Hucky and Buzz are happiest when they
have plans for the day.

What are some of the ways you keep busy?

Be Patient

Hucky and Buzz know that good things happen if they wait.

Try Something Different

Learning new tricks is fun.
What new things will you try?

Slow Down

Hucky and Buzz love racing around, but they know
that taking time to relax is important too.

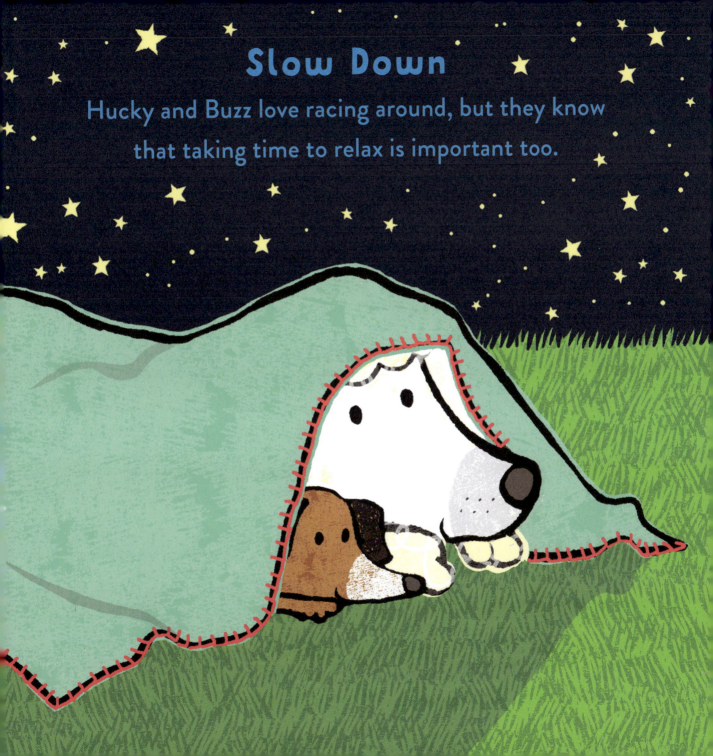